ANCHOR BOOKS

IN THOSE DAYS

Edited by

Heather Killingray

First published in Great Britain in 1999 by
ANCHOR BOOKS
1-2 Wainman Road, Woodston,
Peterborough, PE2 7BU
Telephone (01733) 230761

HB ISBN 1 85930 608 X
SB ISBN 1 85930 603 9

FOREWORD

Anchor Books is a small press, established in 1992, with the aim of promoting readable poetry to as wide an audience as possible.

We hope to establish an outlet for writers of poetry who may have struggled to see their work in print.

The poems presented here have been selected from many entries. Editing proved to be a difficult task and as the Editor, the final selection was mine.

I trust this selection will delight and please the authors and all those who enjoy reading poetry.

Heather Killingray
Editor

CONTENTS

LOOKING BACK TO 30S-40S

Icy cold winters, frosted pictures on windowpanes
Six feet of snow, down country lanes
Three mile walk to school, on dark wet days
Chilblanes, wet feet, drying shoes under school radiators
But so happy, in many ways
The bedrooms were cold, no carpets in those days
Lovely warm fire in living room
Mother waiting for us, after school
With a nice hot meal, children's hour on radio, Ovaltinies
Enid Blyton's 'Sunny Stories' to read
Outside toilet, downstairs through back door
Very cold, to be sure, dry your hair through open oven door
Two or three in a bed, one at bottom, two at the head
But we kept each other warm, in winter's clime
Sunday school, country walks, with mum and dad
Chocolate was hardly ever seen, sweets were rationed
Cocoa was all we had, homemade toffee filled a gap.
Air raids, blackout, shelters underneath the stairs
Until all-clear siren sounded
People were kind and good, doors left open
Rent money on window sill stood
Life was hard, but times were good
With fun for kids, in park and Saturday morning
Picture show, with baited breath, we waited
Tarzan, Roy Rogers, Lassie, she always came home!
Two pence, in front row
When we look back, how we loved it, hardly ever a moan
Mondays washing, took all day! Mothers worked hard
In wartime food was short, clothing too
But, by the grace of God, we all came through.

Irene G Corbett

OUR FIRST HOME

When we got married, fifty years ago,
It was hard, to find a place, to stay,
But we managed, to get an attic,
Just months, before our wedding day.

It had no electricity, or water, in it,
Just a black sink, outside the door,
And it only had, gas lighting,
Also, a very squeaky floor.

Our loo, was shared by four families,
And was on, the outside stair,
But we were young, and so in love,
So we were, very happy there.

But when our daughter was born,
It was something, we had to face,
There was no room, for her pram or cot,
So we had, to find, a bigger place.

Jean Hendrie

THE WAY WE WERE

No teenage Barbie dolls for us
But very much more simple toys
Skipping ropes and hoops for girls
Whip tops and marbles for the boys.

We had horses and carts going on our roads
Not a lorry, a car, or a bus
The roads were quite empty most of the time
So we played there without any fuss.

Tired and happy at the end of the day
In bed in winter without any heat
No hot water bottle whatever the weather
An occasional fire was a very rare treat.

Sweets without wrappers and toffee in trays
Broken up with a hammer for sale
Spanish wood, liquorice and tiger nuts too
And gobstoppers with colours quite pale.

Each shop had its own particular smell
As nothing was pre-packed or sealed
Everything weighed and done up while you wait
So none of the goods were concealed.

The trains were monsters who breathed smoke and fire
Stopping on route for water and coal
With the stoker on-board to get up the steam
These modern diesels have no heart or soul.

No TV to tempt us or pizzas or crisps
No mountain bikes or skateboards for play
But we managed fine and were happy too
Having filled up the whole of the day.

We didn't have time to get bored or sad
I think they were some of the best days we had.

Renie Calcraft

THE WAY WE WERE, 1914-1918

These decades past, memory finds her gaze
Focussed on childhood's scarcely troubled days;
Fortunate group, though war in the balance hung,
Our fathers over age, brothers and friends too young.
My mother's maids, where memories begin,
Taken for granted, friendly, 'living in'.
Later, 'munitions' wages young ones gained
And 'mornings only' older helps remained.
Less hazardous the streets, for cars were few,
And we could walk alone, although we knew
We must not talk to strangers, 'horrid men',
But little cause for fear had parents then.
Butter was rationed, sugar too was short,
But four pence ha'penny a large loaf bought.
Potatoes mixed with flour made heavy bread -
One purple loaf! Then mother baked instead.
Three quarters of a mile we went to school,
In hats and cotton dresses, fresh and cool.
We played upon our way with rope and ball,
With marbles and on 'scooters' - best of all!
Though in our Midland town we'd little fear
Of zeppelins, yet once was danger near.
I woke to sound of bombs - the midnight train
Was followed - but they never came again.
And at my aunt's in London, hardly sound,
More a vibration, shook the air around,
One summer day, about my childish head -
'The guns in Flanders,' so my auntie said.
And yet how happy were those early years,
So little touched by stresses or by fears.

Kathleen M Hatton

NOT LIKE TODAY

A slight rip,
Two ration stamps for sweets laid in my hand.
Not like today.
You can spend what you like.
With my bag of sherbert lemons and humbugs,
I wondered into the scullery,
The backdoor wide open.
'Hello Stanley,'
Mr Pollard said to me.
I watched.
My father and Mr Pollard warming themselves
With the coal fire I had got up early to make.
With my sweets I sat on the back doorstep.
Looking around the scullery,
The brown and green walls,
Making the scullery even more gloomier against the grey morning.
The fresh sausages draped over the kitchen table.
I hear a slight clicking noise,
I followed the noise to the front gate.
A horse and cart had arrived to deliver the milk,
'Me dinner,' my father shouted.
A dog ran past me.

You see Jane,
That's all that happened when you left the back door open.
But now,
I pointed to the paper,
Another burglary,
It was happier in our day,
Not like today.

Joanne Frankham

HARVEST SUPPER

Wheat and barley, oats and rye -
Filling the earth and brimming the eye
With browns and golden shades of yellow,
Fruits all rosy hued and mellow.

The fruit has ripened on the tree,
Now all the fields are clear and free.
The pickers there at break of morn;
Gone are the golden ears of corn.

The harvest is in, Harvest Supper?
Can you hear the organ play?
Hear the laughter, sing the praises.
Give our thanks again this day.

When great shires and man, worked
Side by side, girls ran with baskets
Food piled high, flasks of tea and drinks of ale
Laughing, brown, this harvest time.

Scenic beauty to behold as the autumn
Turns to gold, and plough cuts through
The shaven head, not the great shire
That once did tread . . .

Turning a furrow so straight and clean
Maybe this is how our lives should be -
No false starts or easy moves;
Just arrows ever telling truths.

These are the harvests we must make
Lives made easier, not to break
The hearts of friends who went before
Now waiting on a distant shore.

Bring in your harvest offerings -
Raise your voices, help us sing:
Our thanks and praises to our Lord;
Showing again how much adored.

P Morrill

THE EMPTY COTTAGE

It is standing now empty, old and forlorn
Its walls they are black, the thatch that kept warm,
Adults and children, for many's the year
Is now fading fast, showing its end is near.
Its many's the bucket of whitewash was washed
Yes many's the child in that cottage was washed,
Many's the po that was emptied out
Yes many's the lesson was taught I've no doubt.
The clothes they were washed in a big empty tub
Each Saturday morning, stone floors got a scrub,
The toilet outside was a big open field
With only a ditch, a backside for to shield.
T'was rarely the doors or the windows were locked
The backyard was a home to hens, chickens and cocks,
Back through the years when it was young
Inside those half doors, great work was being done.
On a large open fire, the food it was cooked
In skillets and pots, on a crane they were hooked,
A home to the rambler, youthful and old
In a circle with tea, great stories were told.
A past generation life taught them to grow
In wisdom and kindness, t'was a lot they did know,
At the end of the day, a rosary was said
Thanking God for the living, asking peace for the dead.
Old saying they had like 'God save all here'
In their hearts and their homes, God always seemed near.
The years they have passed, generations have gone
Inside those great walls, fine seeds they were sown
The cottage's now silent, not empty but bare
It's a home to wild, the wee rabbit and hare.

Phil Robinson

THE TIN

In days gone old, in tins so rusted
Was a past left, undusted
Father, mother and the Grands
Paper once held in tender hands
Life is unfolded when you look within
Most of those were trashed in the bin
Rations and stamps to buy what you need
Begged and borrowed and even pleaded
Never enough to go around
But always happiness, I'll be bound
Secret memories left unspoken
But in this tin the spell is broken.
Sorting through a past forgotten
Till I reach the end, the silver bottom
Sad to find the tin now empty
But the table is full of memories plenty
I wish I could ask all the questions behind
But the tin and its family is with angels entwined.

Ann Taplin

PAST TIMES

Born in Bognor to mum and dad, of kids, we numbered eight
Allocated a council house but we shared a garden gate
We were Dolly and Teddy, Wally and Nan, these are our names,
not toys
Len and me, Lulu and Vic, four each of girls and boys.

Brought up in wartime, ration books, doodlebugs flying over
Behind our home were deep tank traps but we played in fields of clover
Outside loo with a bucket, squared newspaper strung on the wall
Dad dug a hole to empty the 'slops', otherwise 'buckets full' was
the call.

Under the table when the sirens wailed, dad would stand at the
open door
Mother would shout and call him a fool, but they wouldn't bomb
him he was sure
The village school just down the street, the school 'marm' was a pain
To swear or misbehave yourself, for that, you'd get the cane.

At the village shop mum could buy 'on tick' big pram and kids in tow
Then clean and scrub to earn a crust, pay up, when she'd got the dough
Dad would drink at the village pub, sway home later than sooner
Mum would know he was on this way home, by his singing
'Lily of Laguna',

Sometimes she would take us all to the pub, to get him back home,
they would talk
If he was too drunk he'd sit in the pram, all us poor kids had to walk
There were other times he didn't come home, our Sunday lunch ready
And so down to the pub, 'his dinner on plate', see him propping the bar,
and she'd throw.

The pub's still there, dad passed on, some forty years ago
Mum then went but our 'home' still stands, and to look at it sometimes,
I know that comparing life, with how we lived then and how we all
live now.
Those times were hard, especially for mum, but I think they were
better somehow.

Joan Bourner

WHAT USED TO BE:

This is how it used to be . . .
Some today remember what lots call,
'The good old days'
Without harm kids played out in the street,
Looking forward to Saturday's toffee treat.

We were wartime children,
Very young, but remember the valid ration book,
Lots that were needed from the shops,
This was a very important thing people took.

Yet there was fairness . . .
There was glee, everyone was so friendly,
Doors left open, while folks slipped next door,
For a coffee and chat . . . that seems not any more.

We used to watch the old train,
Passing the end of the garden it came,
Hooting and tooting, blowing out smoke,
Even that has gone, it is no joke,
As now houses there be,
The one time railway line, no longer to see.

Then went the pound and ten bob note,
The half crown, now it is decimals you quote,
Less wages, cheaper things, you need not guess,
Yes, even the milk and your daily bread.

You who are the children today,
May laugh at what I say, but mark these words,
Even you in time will see differences,
As into adults you turn, and in what does occur.

That is when you yourselves . . .
Will start to look back on things that used to be,

In your 'one time good old days', 'God bless you all'.

Anita M Slattery

WIGAN 1913

(This is the first part of a 102 line poem written as one of a group of poems in 1987 by Annie J Major - who died shortly after)

I was born in a house in a quiet Wigan street.
  A long terraced row all so tidy and neat.
The houses were small - just two up and two down,
  Two small windows in front and a door painted brown.
We had no bathroom of course but we did not mind.
  Our large old tin bath just suited us fine.
Then hot and cold water poured in with delight,
  Many elbows dipped in to make sure it was right.
The old fashioned fireplace just looking a treat -
  Thanks to Brasso and Zeebo and, of course, elbow grease.
The firelight would glitter on the black oven door,
  On the fender and brasses all bright and aglow.
Our small house was lit only by gas of course,
  And the mantles were fragile and easily broke.
It was a routine trip to the corner shop
  For a new gas mantle in its square paper box.
The snag was to get it back home in one piece.
  We usually made it with a sigh of relief.
We had a small kitchen - just a pantry in fact.
  And a shallow brown sink near the door with a latch.
The back yard had a wash-house down to the right;
  A boiler for wash days always a terror to light.
At the end of the yard a closet next to the gate.
  So handy when you left things in a little bit late.
Behind the door, on a nail, there was always a pad
  Of small squares of newspaper cut up by my dad.
We had two narrow entries that led round to the backs -
  The back's - just a yard or two of solid dirt track,
Then quite a steep slope we called Fisher's brew.
  Which gave the boys chance to try something new.

A J Major 1978

THE WAY WE WERE

Doodlebugs droning over roof tops
Crashing, flashing that never stops
Vimto, toffee apples, little corner shops
That's the way we were.

Coal fires roaring in sooty hearths
Children splashing in cold tin baths
We were not very rich, but we had lots of laughs
That's the way we were.

Loos resting in spooky backyards
Newspaper squares hanging like cards
Smoking roll-ups were completely barred
That's the way we were.

Things worth remembering was dripping on toast
Families enjoyed their Sunday roast
Walking to see defences on the coast
That's the way we were.

School knickers puckering, sagging at the side
Bottle green or navy blue, and very, very wide
Parachute silk for the blushing bride
That's the way we were.

Heavy on rationing was meats, sweets and cheese
Sugar, dried eggs, coffee and teas
At least we had a few tins of mushy peas
That's the way we were.

Happy singing round a piano in the local pub
Granny with camphorated oil, giving chests a rub
Honey and lemon in an old brown jug
That's the way we were.

How about bringing back those forgotten years
Where children could play happily without any fears
Drugs had no place, it was safe for old dears
That's the way we were.

Brenda Moore

THE WAY WE WERE

The way we were
Children were seen and not heard
Manners were the order of the day
Politics you thought about
But were not for you to say

O dear if we were late for dinner
With shy look we would sit
Please let me grow up quickly
Never will I have to eat those awful green things
That were so good for me

Eager to leave the table
O dear I did bang that door
Where were my manners
Maybe children are right
Freedom is the way they think

Wanting to grow up quickly
Staying out late
Homework last on your mind
Never to hear 'Why did you get home so late?'

Freedom was a dream
Why cannot I appreciate
The way things were.

Frances Abrahart

THE WAY WE WERE

After my 65 years in life, so much has changed -
Could be better - or could be worse!
Granny and auntie lived next door -
And the cousins came and slept happily on the floor.
We as children went out to play -
And I remember the gas meters took just 1d per day -
The price of gas is not that today.
Our fathers worked hard for little pay.
Mother baked bread and washed clothes for friends -
They had to make ends meet to pay their way.
They scrimped and saved before World War II
We remember the ration books and Digging for Victory.
Our street was a family, with very good neighbours -
It was never a crime to borrow or lend!
Nobody bothered to lock up the back door -
Grandad played his old piano at Christmas and someone sang.

Sunday's dinner was not a roast -
Perhaps sheep's head broth and potato cakes
And we loved the cakes that granny baked!
Rice pudding and treacle pie or pobbies for a sweet -
It was only Christmas dinner that was a treat.
On Christmas Eve grandad would pluck the fowl -
Feathers were flying everywhere, this made granny growl!
Not many indoor games and parties like that - no not now -
Because life has improved so much.
There's computers, television and such,
So, why, with life so better in so many ways -
Do I think of those times as 'good old days'.

M E Smith

RHYMING CHAT

It doesn't matter what you have done or where you have been,
it is what you are today. I would like to tell you a funny story about
my tin bath, if I may.
My mother bought a house with three floors, semi-basement,
upper ground. I moved in the top three rooms and landing, there I
found the water pipes reached to the top of the stairs to an Ascot by
the sink, the small bedroom housed the cooker, a slight muddle
don't you think?
One night, when I came home from the pub
Went round the back, from the hook took the tub
With arms upstretched did a coalman's lift,
Round three short flights, the walls it 'biffed'
To the top landing in front of the sink
The hosepipe fitted to the Ascot, all in a wink!
A small smell of gas, there was no flue.
Sitting in the water hot then came a voice I knew
My son and his three friends came home
Just when I thought I was all alone!
'Step over me muvver, she's having a bath'
They dutifully did, but they did not laugh
At least they remembered to shut their door
Before they drank beer and played cards on the floor
I baled it out and took it down in the morning
Went to work, then much later, without any warning
The building trade mid bricks and mortar,
It was mother's tin bath, they were after!
Sure enough in my son's van
Went my tin bath, still useful to man
To mix his plaster, I must confess
My old tin bath was passing the test
We don't live in that house anymore
I wonder if the new people lock the back door?

June Barber

WHAT I MISS

It wasn't the kiss
And it wasn't the pain of missing him,
Nor was it the memories left undone.
It wasn't the scars he showed me;
Felt like I needed to heal.
But it was more the raw fact
I no longer needed him.

Wasn't the longing I'd felt found in his soul!
Or the bond we'd made that seemed so *long* ago.
It couldn't have been the things he said to me,
Or even the love he showed.
But now I was left standing on my own.

It was never the hours we spent
Or even the way our hearts could melt.
It wasn't the crack of the whip - that it felt like leaving him
Just the pure gone fact that I didn't need him now.
I'll always care for him - somehow.

Naomi Elisa Price

I REMEMBER WORLD SO FINE

I remember world
so fine
long before
this present time
was in its final prime.

When skies were
truly
innocently blue
with crystals and sapphires
gladly shining through.

When birds of wonder
glided playfully
in loving rays
of golden sun's embrace
drinking cheerfully
living sparks of celestial
light
- in their never-ending flight -
from
fountain
or the everlasting
divine fire
glittering
like precious diamond lace
in
fairy princess' glorious
tiara.

Rorone

UNTITLED

Times were hard in the 'good old days'
When the outside loo seemed like miles away
In actual fact fourteen concrete steps we had to go down
The loo was about one hundred yards away
A bucket in one hand almost full from overnight family use
You finally got there to join the queue
You could be at the end of a line of twenty-two
For there were other families in that cul-de-sac
All waiting to hurry back
Neighbours took their turn to clean the loo
And supply squares of newspaper held by a screw
We moved on to something better
An inside loo and a bath we treasured
The yuppies frowned and screamed
How dare they put such scum so near to them?
But the folks from the slums rose above it all
Their children graduated to level with the snobs
They showed their pride and held their heads up high
The snobs were amazed that the environment
Could change a whole population to rise.

Nan Hawkins

120 YEARS DESTROYED

To you our teachers past and present,
You made us what we are,
We stand in confidence and pride.
As Penrhosians, we will never fall.

For every brick within our school,
A heart and tear is filled.
For every book, desk and chair
A memory fulfilled.

To you the principle of our school,
You say you will re-home us,
With which we don't deny,
But how do you plan to surround us
With a century of memories and history behind us?

We may fall out with other people,
But together, we will stand,
Together, when you take our hearts and tears,
Destroy our buildings too.

But as Penrhosians we will stand
Through and through.

Gemma Steele (12)

Childhood Memories Of How Life Was

I was born in a farmhouse, with a roof of thatch
The door was never locked, it was left on the latch.
A family of twelve, three children to a bed
Not much room but we were all well fed.
Hard boiled or soft, from ducks or hens, we would never tire
Of eggs boiled for breakfast, boiled on a big turf fire.
With a long handled fork we toasted the bread
And with home-made butter it was thickly spread.
With plenty of cow's milk in a mug or bowl of tea
Then with our 'piece' in our satchel, we set off to school with glee.
With wellies on, if wet, or leather boots, if dry
The child left behind would howl and cry.
We walked or ran along the puddled, muddy lane
We knew we had chores to do when we got home again.
Sometimes we got a ride with ol' Harry, in the cart
He sometimes sang or whistled and sometimes he'd fart!
We had a teacher and a master at our public elementary school
The ruler and the cane ensured we kept to rule.
The ruler rapped our knuckles, the cane slapped our hands
If we children didn't obey all the commands.
Around the blackboard we stood to chant our timetables
And read aloud in turn from books of facts and fables.
School was quite a happy place, lots of children and space
At noon we ate our 'piece' and around the school we'd race.
We played football, cricket, tig and skipping
When it snowed we had great fun sliding and slipping.
Having to go outside in the cold and wet was hard
To the 'dry' lavatories in a corner of the yard.
Innocent children accepting the ways of life, as it came
The way we were, forming characters, life's now a different game.

Anne Haire

THE WHEAT FIELD

Glinting in the late sun's glow
A swelling, golden sea of wheat,
Each heavy head sways to and fro
And the air smells very sweet.

Rippling in the silver moonlight
With dancing, whiskered silhouettes,
Whispering on the still of night
Sharing the harvest mouse's secrets.

Comes the dawn an early rising
Harvest helpers to the field,
Fine the weather for the scything
Plentiful, the good earth's yield.

Shimmering in the heat of day
The harvest prayer is granted,
Carefully tended in every way
Since the seed was planted.

Now 'tis time to down the tine
The stock to lean back on,
To disband, with cheese and wine
And make merry, the day is won.

J M Rosson Gaskin

WATCHING FROM A WINDOW

As I watch the planes from above,
And the school I once knew,
I think of 1938 when the school was still standing,
And no planes in the sky.
I watched from my window,
While my parents were killed,
There they lay in the dirt,
Blood running from their bodies.
I was sent away,
It wasn't home,
It had no bombs,
Or planes.
Instead it had meadows,
And fresh air which engulfed my lungs.
This place was unwelcome,
And cruel.
I ran away never to return,
I met another stray like me.
We met new people,
And saw new places,
But it ended and we were caught.
We were taken to another place.
This place was kind and loving,
But I seem to be the devil's son,
Bringing sadness to all places.
As I watched from a far off window,
That kind and loving place was no more,
And no more of my friend Max.
I was moved like a bag of luggage to another place,
Which was kind and loving like before,
And here I am still remembering the war.

Emily Havis (12)

GIVE FAITH TO THE YOUNG OF TODAY

Now our age is passing, with shadows falling fast,
Depicting the ages we cast,
The church is shadowed, lonely,
The pubs are bombing on,
The young like robots wander,
A cavalcade of unknown valour,
Buried in selfishness,
Their faith, dim, burning, sallow,
Their parents at the helm, let go,
For their young ones drift unguided,
With the Lamp of Faith, so low,
Oh how dark, how dark this decade,
That man alone, has shadowed made,
Light, light, the Star of Faith, for the young,
At the Altar stair,
And steer now, the next generations,
In faith and prayer.
Let the light of His faith now light the world,
So that when the generations to come,
Look back and read of our age,
They will bless the light that shone, out upon our stage,
Let the voice of man ring, with the blessings of his God,
Let him sing loudly the hymns,
Our forefathers sang and give to our children, the hope,
That faith alone can give, these sacred gifts, bequeathed to man,
Love, joy, laughter and faith,
Born to the young on the wings of prayer,
From Earth to Heaven, through prayer.
Yes, give faith, to the young today.

B D S Leith

THE WAY WE WERE

Look at the world
how it used to be,
how people lived and
used to speak,
the world that carried
politeness and it also
had respect,
people who cared for one another
and they cared until death,
but now the world has changed,
in a very terrible way,
people have turned to evil
and lost what they had once
gained,
the happiness, the joy
flipped fast as a coin,
greediness and hatred
filled in people's brains,
now we think will the
world ever be the same
again!

Fatima Jamshad (16)

DOWN THE YARD

When I was very small
We didn't have toilet rolls at all
A square cut from the daily news
Was used when we had done our poohs
It was our duty without fail
To cut these squares from the Daily Mail
Thread them on a string, like a little book
And hang them onto a small hook
As each sheet was pulled away
A wad of paper there would stay
Held up by the bit of string
And with a finger I would ping
The bits would fly into the air
And for a moment they'd stay there
Then they'd float down to the ground
And lie there, all strewn around
It wasn't paper but birds in flight
An aeroplane or a paper kite
A little man with a parachute
He always landed on my boot
So I'd jump and stamp on him and say
Sorry, old chap, it's not your day
What fantasies a child's mind plays
But they were happy, happy days
Couldn't do it now though chum
You'd end up with a big black bum.

Evelyn Ward

THE WAY WE WERE

Some people think we 'oldies' queer
When we harp back to yesteryear
But in many, many, many ways
They really were the good old days
You could leave your door off the lock
People's word was as firm as Gibraltar Rock
You could leave your front door open
For the baker, the butcher or grocer
But could you do that now?
The answer is 'No sir, no sir, no sir'
You could leave your windows open
And never give a care!
But if you left them open now
You'd find the cupboard bare!
Most were as poor as the proverbial mouse
We laboured hard for the bit that we got
We dug our gardens in the good old days
Didn't use pesticides or obnoxious sprays
Which upset the balance of things
Especially those glorious birds on the wing
Now they're left unattended, many a tree
And many a bush
We've lost that stunner, our beautiful thrush
I end this slightly sad little tale
And think of our songbird
As he 'bashed up' his snail.

C R Crawford

THE WAR YEARS

Yes! I remember Mr Chamberlain signed a Treaty
for peace for us all.
That meant nothing to the Germans as I recall!
Little children suffered, some of them had to leave Mum and Dad,
They were evacuated to the country - all were very sad.
Food was rationed, Mum had quite a job to do!
Providing meals for me and for you.
The siren's screaming filled us with fear!
For they sounded to warn us, enemy planes were near!
Why can't we humans live in peace and harmony?
I quite often wonder - it is all beyond me . . .

Sheila K A Thompson

THE WAY WE WERE
The Wisdom Of Fear Or (The Cessation Of Crime).

As scientific knowledge floods the passing years
We almost take for granted each wonder that appears.
Despite these great inventions surely one must ask
Are we really happy or still groping in the dark?
A hundred years ago we treasured drugs when ill
But now black-market scoundrels sell quantities that kill!
So many things so glorious are converted into vice
Which their makers viewed quite surely as something really nice.

In the days of Queen Victoria one could give a child a smack
But now our foolish rulers through the common-sense they lack.
Have said this wise correction is no longer making sense
And that's why youthful plunder these days is so intense.
An Islam priest has told us his crime-free land has proved
That nothing is so frightening as thieving hands removed.
This brutal form of treatment would not suit us over here
But let us not stay thoughtless about the power of fear.
There is no need for Moslems to be locking up their cars.
For a thief with lust for stealing would suffer frightful scars.

To us these deadly punishments are cruel and very queer
But once again they show us the valid power of fear.
The kindly way we treat a thief is utterly beyond belief.
If brought back the days of stocks
Not one of us would suffer shocks.
Foul louts don't mind a stretch in gaol
It's time to note the way we fail.
We'd like to see strict rules appear
That recognise the power of fear.
Let those who cause the old dire dread
Be crushed and bullied well instead . . .

Colin H Cattley

NOSTALGIC EVOCATIONS
Word Pictures In Aroma, Sight and Sound

In childhood - frog's spawn, tadpoles, butterfly nets.
Crystal sets, cat's whisker and earphones, Rover, Beano,
Dandy, Hotspur, Film Fun comic papers.
On the wireless - Children's Hour and one-legged Uncle Mac -
'Goodnight children everywhere!'
The Railway Children, The Swish of the Curtain, Toy Town,
Larry the lamb, Denis the dachshund, Mr Growser and the
unforgettable signature tune.
Burnt milk indicating bedtime.
Long summer evenings. Short winter snow covered days.
Coal fires in bedrooms. Wooden rollers and cast iron mangles,
squeezing washing soda into galvanised bath beneath.
The sweet smell of damp American oilcloth held with rusty
drawing pins on scrubbed kitchen table.

In World War II - 'Boots circulating library', moaning claxton
siren. Anderson shelter dripping with condensation and snuffed
out candle wax. Air raids, incendiary bombs, anti-aircraft fire.
The black-out *'put that light out'!* Air raid wardens, gas masks in
cardboard boxes, strung around neck - 'never to be caught without',
soldiers billeted
American *'Yanks'* filling the dance hall with 'Sweet Caporal' cigarettes
and smart uniforms.
Telegrams - *'with regret',* Red Cross Prisoner of War notification.
Civilian casualty list. The sound of enemy aircraft overhead vibrating
the out of window zinc meat safe - forerunner of the *fridge.*

In the High Street - Sainsbury's mahogany marble top counters.
Bentwood chairs for customers to watch butter patted into greaseproof
paper packets. 'Overhead tramway' to accounts office with loose change
in Ski-lift canister all at a pull-on chain. The draper's and dressmaker's
shop with two and eleven three pence or a packet of pins
in lieu of three farthings. Money of some weight which felt its worth.
A twist of boiled sweets in newspaper cornucopias. The irongmonger
seeped in paraffin and beeswax. The corn merchant's sacks of feed
rolled down like elephant's socks at back edge of pavement. The

retractable shop awning.

The village shop and post office.

Few motor cars at kerbside.

Flannels and sports coats allowed by staff on Saturday mornings only, in the high street bank, otherwise dark suit. No females on counter.

The poetic list is endless, the sights, sounds and smells linger in the mind.

No spotless hygienic supermarkets with canned music and bumping trolleys emptied into car boots crammed with frozen foots. *'No dogs except Guide Dogs'.*

'A way of life - long gone'!

Then we had time to be happy . . .

Howard Trevor Gaunt

WAR-BOYS

The boys went to the boxing ring down at the local fair,
They saw the ref set up the fights and blood fly through the air.
Ronnie beat the champion, no challenger would fight
'Til his brother saw his chance to prove his mother's sayings right.

His back was crimson with the knuckles of his bother's beating
His head was pounding low and steady with the canvas heaving.
The bell was sounded sharp and clear to warn of Mrs Kray,
Hitting, punching, gouging, jabbing those standing in her way.

She knelt between the flailing fists and begged her boys for peace,
'Til now they'd only known the toys of war, the rations lease
'If you want to fight, fight *them* out there!' she screamed at both
                                                            her sons
The crowd was hushed, 'If you two fight then only *they* have won.'

'Death and heartache lives within us now, war's ruined all our lives'
'And love and hope and faith boys, it's no *crime* that you survived!'
'For you, my boys, are boys of war - spectators to the hearse'
'This ring is like the world, my boys, it's *fear* that steals the purse.'

A punch was thrown, again she screamed 'Who'd love you as much
                                                            as *me?*'
So *fear* is power thought they and power is *love* thought we.
At her grave we bowed in sorrow at the memory of that day,
War, hunger, power, love and love alone, through Mrs Kray.

Scarlett-Barley Robinson

THE WAY WE WERE
(A Child's Love)

So this is love, so they say
This feeling in my heart.
I always wondered what it was
Right from the very start.
I thought it's licking a lollipop
Until your mouth ran dry.
But mother says I'm foolish
Just trying to be coy.
Coy! Another word to get me in a fix
I think I'll heed my father
You know I'm only six!

Years have gone and I'm now full grown,
And still this feeling stays
Within my heart, like as before
The yesterdays and toady's.
Mother looks at father,
They both exchange a grin.
Now I know what love is
For love comes from within!

Joyce Morrish

THE WAY WE WERE

The *good old days*
The *way we were*
In *days of yore.*
My mind lingers more
On the leisurely style,
That prevailed all the while.
In bygone days,
But mixed with the good,
There was plenty of bad,
That made people sad!
Facilities may have been primitive,
But then industry used its initiative.
So present day living took
A turn for the better.
But *Stop! Look! Listen!*
Although present day life
Is free of old day strife,
There is a serious problem.
I believe it to be
The disruptive TV.
Mental health of countless folk
Are at risk with TVs information bloke.
TV - the root of much stress
When viewers' absorb the political mess.
Murders, horror, rape as well
All is gist to the TV well.
Gathered from far and near
To distress the populace in the ear.
The *good old days* - gone forever
But *present days* are not that clever!

F W Leedham

INNOCENT LAND

White cotton wool balls
Mixed with gossamer silk
Perched atop the rolling green hills
Bringing back memories of forgotten times.

Times when man looked after the land
Times when women took care of the men
Days when children played freely around
Secure in the knowledge that no harm would come.

Gone are those days when people were free
Gone the days when children were safe
Now in our time all we can do
Is look to the hills and recall yesteryear.

Fiona Higgins

STOKE-ON-TRENT

Stone
black stone
lintels black
murky blue walls
lead tinted red
ashen
ingrained
diaries of sweat.

Soil
black soil
miners' bread
the country's wealth
awash.

Smog heavy air
slack hills
once black
now green
reminders of
pollution.

High
sky high
chimney stacks
bulging kilns
grandfather's skills
wanted.

Coal face
faces black
sandwich boxes
white smiles
mates
missus waiting.

Work was plentiful!

Helga Hopkinson

MEMORY LANE

A stroll down memory lane,
Unrolling my history scroll,
Recounting the way we were,
Reliving my childhood again.

A humble cottage, an open door,
Sawdust on a flagstone floor,
A simmering pot on a kitchen range,
A purring cat on a peg-rag mat.

Home made bread, chamber pots under the bed,
(Just for emergency use - no bathroom or indoor loo's)
A primitive outdoor *privvy*
A scrub in a galvanised tub,
Hung on a wall in the yard, a cold water tap
No hot water geyser, no fridge and no freezer.

Puritan, Sunlight and Carbolic soap,
Flat irons warmed on the hob,
Ready to cope with the ironing job,
A cockerel crowing at dawning,
Hen's laying eggs every morning.
A squeaky old rocking chair,
Children reciting a prayer.

A ticking Grandfather clock,
Knitting gloves and darning socks,
The sound of a tinkling piano
Mother singing soprano.
Remembered joy - forgotten care,
Two parents with time to spare.
Counting our blessings,
Just to be there
Happy - the way we were.

Mary G Kane

HOW CAN YOU UNDERSTAND?

How can you understand, who were not here,
The love we bore our then still sovereign land?
Joined in a common unity of aim,
Before today's schisms, which sunder us apart,
We worked together through each day's routine,
Then took our turn beneath the silent stars
To watch for fires when the night raiders came.

The day France fell, when every following train
Brought silent remnants of a defeated force,
Brothers in arms, though speaking alien tongues,
Whose pain we shared - we clearly understood
Only these isles, flanked by the narrow sea,
Still held a hope of final victory.
How can you understand, who were not here?

The odds impossible, the chips high stacked,
Nightly unsure what a new day might bring,
Daily expectant of an invading force
That never came, we laughed at wartime jokes,
Grumbled at shortages, spent leaves too short
Followed by separations all too long,
When letters formed a tenuous link of love.
How can you understand, who were not here?

What's hardly won should be more highly prized.
When through our summer skies the ceaseless roar
Of engines overhead gave waited news
Of counterstrikes, with expectation high
We should win through; then in the final peace
The Church bells rang, not with a danger warning
But in full joy; and dancing filled the streets,
And homes rejoiced to welcome those returning.
How can you understand, who were not here,
The love we bore our wounded sovereign land?

Iris Smith

SEVENTIES' MUM

How glad I am of these precious days spent
Before school system on you made claim.
Fast fleeting days that came and went
Never to be repeated; Never the same!
Yet memories remain, golden - in my mind,
Not far away or hard to find.
Of warm little arms and soft little cheek,
The love, the laughter
I just close my eyes to seek.
Stories read by fireside warm,
Of Corduroy and Blackberry Farm.
Chicken Licken or Billy Goat Gruff,
You knew them by heart but never enough.
Sunny days too, in field and lane,
Or Play Area seesaw and swing.
I walk there now and remember those times
Only echoes of children's voices ring.
Deserted now no one goes there to play,
This is another time- another day!
The old fallen tree dragged away,
In fear a child being hurt they say.
Gnarled old log where we tied the dog.
No more allowed there anyway.
A penalty of a hundred pounds
If evidence of canine found!
Yet sandpit where small fat hands safety sifted.
Hazardous now should be shifted,
All beer cans and traces of teenage passion spent,
Before innocence could take hold it seems - it went.
Grasses that whispered on the breeze,
On lazy summer afternoons droned with visiting bees.
Today sings a different tune,
It pulsates now with heavy rock.
From joyriders by light of moon.
Drivers of cars not their own
Stolen from someone else's home.

Accompanied by helicopter with heat-seeking light,
Yes! This is another time - another night!
Grateful I am to have been a seventies mom,
With flowing skirt and flowers in my hair,
And dreams of peace in a perfect world.
Where man could freely love and share.
But glad I am of those days with you,
For the memories remain
And the love stays true.

Y Liggins

POST-WAR REMINISCENCES

In the village of my childhood
Was an enterprising grocer,
Who sold food to everybody,
Cigarettes, and sweets to children.
And because it had been wartime
Folk could not get petrol coupons,
So they could not drive their cars far.
They bought their food in the village,
From the butcher, baker, grocer
And the local farmers also.
At the grocer's there were biscuits.
They were all in tins, the biscuits,
And they could be bought so cheaply.
There were also broken biscuits.
These were retailed, but much cheaper,
So that many people bought them.
Because we were short of paper,
At the shop they put the sugar
(We could only have two ounces)
Into a cone made of paper
Which they had a knack of folding
So that it would hold two ounces,
Even of granulated sugar,
And not one grain would be wasted.
If one bought a bottled soft drink
And one brought the empty back, one
Could get threepence on the bottle.
These are some things I remember
From the village of my childhood.

Jillian Mounter

CHANGING TIMES

We have all heard the stories,
Of the *good old days,*
From parents and relations
In all sorts of ways.

You never had it so good!
That was often said.
They only had simple games,
Then were sent to bed.

Times have changed so very much
In so many ways.
Some for better, some for worse,
Some simply amaze!

As I marvel at the change,
Since my early years.
I must confess I cannot help
But shed a few tears.

The streets were safer places then,
Places just to play in.
Doors could be left *on the latch!*
Without fear of a break-in.

The hi-tech world we live in,
Is taken for granted.
Videos, mobiles, computers,
And such - all accepted.

What of the future for all,
Children and grandchildren?
We can but hope they keep the values
Handed down to them!

T Daley

THE WAY WE WERE

Although folk don't think much of the good old days,
Climbing hurdles, as we had to; helped in many ways.
One of the finest lessons learnt during the war,
Was how to live amicably together - be we rich or poor!

Just having left my school,
I was often to find how life could pall.
You were too young to enter the vocation of choice,
And when quiet asked why you couldn't find a voice.

I have two sisters older than me
One joined the Air Force, the other the Land Army.
But I remember the Air Ships very well,
For it was often on the children that they fell!

You see when there was any cutting back to be done
And elders insisted on their bit of fun
It was usually the younger ones that would suffer,
They were considered a very useful buffer!

The day the National Service was cut,
We were all very thankful - but
Many felt this was not the way
To help all to a more peaceful day.

Betty Green

AMY (MAID OF ALL WORK)

Ruddy, round faced, apple-cheeked Amy.
Eldest of eight and just fifteen.
Employed by a city-dweller,
For meagre pay, to cook and clean.

Sturdy, willing - fenland Amy,
Reared on flat and cloying sod,
Side by side she stooked with Father,
Sat by Mum in the House of God.

Loyal, trusting, joyful Amy
Elbows in the glazed sink deep,
Scouring pans in rainbow bubbles,
Stacking pots in an ordered heap.

Up at five to riddle ashes,
Practical pinafore - neck to knee;
After luncheon, black dress, white cap,
Frilled with lace to serve the tea.

Her domain the stone floored scullery.
Rooflight raised to free the steam,
Copper in the farthest corner,
Creel attached to wooden beam.

Humming; *Red sails in the sunset.*
Singing lyrics of the day,
Gentle, generous, loving Amy,
With winning ways and time for play.

I, as a toddler, sought the kitchen
Sat on her broad knees, held so tight.
Smelled the scent of bread and beeswax
Warmed my toes by the coal-fire bright.

Audrey Shaw

THE WAY WE WERE

'We are at war with Germany!'
The words meant nothing to me.
At fourteen years I was just a child
Growing up in a world that was free.

My life was about to be transformed
From heaven to almost hell.
German bombers flew over our home each night
Causing noise from our gunners' shells.

We carried our gas masks to school each day
And in shelters did most of our work.
Old *Adolph* was not going to stand in our way
For our learning we would not shirk.

Dad, in the Navy - was doing his bit
So Mum had to hold the fort.
She prayed that the *doodle-bugs* wouldn't hit
Our house in their nightly sport.

Our food was scarce so we all got thin.
Few sweets and no fruit to be seen.
The U-boats would not let our food ships in
So we had to make use of our green.

Each scrap of grass was tilled and raked
So we could grow food instead.
We tried for a while to eat whale steaks
And baked our own home-made bread.

Though London took some heavy flak
Our spirits were held high.
Our bombers paid the Nazis back
And we beat them in the sky.

Although I remember the way we were
I pray that those days will never recur!

Helen Strangwige

THE LITTLE SHED DOWN THE GARDEN

I well remember the little shed, at the bottom of the garden,
'twas known to us as the 'Kludgy'; if you will beg my pardon,
It was surrounded by a privet hedge, but not a pretty sight
and going down there after dark, the candle you had to light,

The inside was all whitewashed, and the box seat just planed wood,
in the front there was a little door, behind which the bucket stood.
Dad was away in the Army, there were two sisters, and I the only son,
and every time that bucket was full; Oh yes, I was the lucky one,

I had to get the garden spade, and in a marked spot dig a hole,
and take that bucket and empty it; not to be seen by a living soul
I was only six years old at the time, so the contents splashed about,
I wonder if that's the reason why, I now suffer with chronic gout.

The hole filled in and levelled off, and the next marker put in place,
my shoes and socks would be put in soak, then wash my hands and
face,
The old tin bath would be taken in, and placed in front of the fire,
whilst mother was getting it filled, I would remove my other attire,
Those old tin baths were deadly, they would give you quite a shock,
one side was freezing cold, but the side nearest the fire was red hot.

One day we had a posh lady visit, and she needed to go to the 'loo',
we gave her a general description, and told her what she should do,
She came running from the garden, saying 'There's no lock
on the door'
I told her not to worry, we hadn't lost a bucket in five years or more,

In '47 we moved to a new house, with flushing toilet and a patio too,
I thought it unhygienic then, with some of the strange things we had to
do,
The day of our house-warming party, we held a mammoth barbecue,
so now we were cooking outside; but going into the house for the loo.

How nice it would be to go back in time, to relive those days of old,
they must have been special times, or these stories would not be told,
When you speak to senior citizens, they love to talk of yesteryear,
hard times maybe, but happy ones; saying 'That's the way we were'.

Wenn The Penn

ALIVE AT FORTY-FIVE

Helter skelter to the shelter
At the sound of the siren's wail
Our broken sleep, would make us weep
Wondering when peace would prevail

My sister, brother, and mother
One bunk, and a little armchair
Mother prayed, in her gentle way
She believed, God was with us in there

Our heat and light, came through the night
From a little battered oil lamp
In blankets wrapped, we sometimes napped
For our refuge was cold and damp

Songs we'd sing, and mother would bring
Laughter, funny stories galore!
Widowed in prime, at a bad time
We children, were all she lived for

Through the years, of laughter and tears
Many nocturnal trips we made
Though life was tough, as we grew up
Foundations of love mother laid

At last! Came peace, and happy release
In the year nineteen forty-five
We prayed, and cried, for those who died
And thanked God, we were still alive!

Patricia Whittle

The Way We Were

In the good old days of long ago
What happiness we shared
We had no riches of this world
But parents who loved and cared

We walked to school, brought a
Turf for the fire
Learnt our lessons with slate
And chalk
Ate our lunch of soda bread
Of school dinners there was no talk
Home from school we had our work
Feeding the hens and bringing in the eggs
Bringing tea to our father ploughing
In the fields
Gathering potatoes hoping for good yields.

And when the day was over
We gathered round the hearth
A big turf fire was burning bright
As we had our supper by candlelight
Then the latch would lift of our
Unlocked door 'God bless all here' our
Neighbour would say
And take out his accordion and start to play

We hadn't much money but we
Had what would do
We had no bathroom just an outside loo
We carried the water from a spring well
We had no fridges, no electricity
No washing machines
But I would love to go back
To the time of my dreams.

Brigid Quinn

INCH MILES

Literate and six,
I cast about for print and, finding none
In that albeit joyous, kindly home
Save cereal packets and
One unexpected notebook,
I studied both.

The Puffed Wheat pack
Whereon I noticed first
The prevalence and functions of the letter e
Afforded text from which I crystallised the
English language spelling rules.

Different trove
Was printed on the notebook back.

Number facts in sumptuous words -
Ten chains one furlong, eight furlongs to the mile,
Four pecks one bushel
And in a pint, four gills -

Subsumed by that mouth-watering word
The unexplained and glorious avoirdupois,
Ordered the world,

Helped me select the jugs
To carry to the churn
For filling from a two gill cup
With milk to scald for yellow cream.

Today, a second eager six year old
At carpet boules
After his weekly spelling lesson,
Asked me for a metre rule to check who'd won.

Instead I gave him my accustomed wand,
A fine brass-ended yardstick.

Dorothy Pope

SUCKING HUMBUGS

'We never heard of single mothers,'
One old dear declared
'A shameful thing in our day,
No, we never would have dared'

'Disgraceful's what I call it'
Her companion sniffed disgust
'Depraved, the youngsters these days
And encouraged in their lust'

'Yes, the contraceptives they have now
And money from the state,
It's the children I feel sorry for . . .
What they must tolerate'

They sat there sucking humbugs
As our bus splashed through the rain
And after but a moment's pause
They started up again

'That Maureen Brown's a dark horse though,
I saw her just last week
At Freda Cooper's funeral
And we got a chance to speak

It seems she has a son!
Got herself pregnant at sixteen
And all these years we never knew
It shocked me, well, I mean . . .

Her family were mortified
They sent her to an aunt
Says she fought to keep the baby
But they told her, 'Well, you can't!'

Adopted by some awful folk
Apparently he was
He told a sorry tale
About his childhood out in Oz

They rang the bell to stop the bus
And stepped into the rain
My watch showed I'd be late
For ante-natal class again.

Kim Montia

MODERN CONVENIENCES

I remember our outside toilet, what a pain,
It had to be visited in sun, wind or rain.
Until I was eighteen my parents lived like this,
But then a bathroom was installed at last, what bliss!
No more bathing in front of the sitting room hearth,
After filling up antiquated tin bath.
Finally, we'd got modern gadgets in our place,
We were the same as the rest of the human race.

Susan Mullinger

YESTERDAY

Memories of my childhood,
come back in many ways,
I often wish I could return
to those sweet easy days,

Whip-n-top and Hula hoops,
poppet beads to link,
Gob stoppers and Rainbow drops
and playing Tiddlywinks,

Liquorice sticks and Black Jacks,
rounders in the street,
Shiny brand new roller-skates,
adorning tiny feet,

Rolling marbles in the yard,
Tag and kiss-catch too,
Always busy with my friends
so very much to do,

Remembering those happy times
of innocents at play,
Our games so very simple,
belong to yesterday.

Joyce Costello

REMEMBER

Remember how we walked along
Our bare feet touched the earth.
Recall the sparrows that we saw
Just moments after birth.

Remember when we climbed the hill
To see the other side,
And then that field of buttercups
Where we would play and hide.

Remember too the willow tree
Where we would make our den;
The little stream that tumbled by
and then on through the Glen.

Remember how we used to bathe
And splash down in the loch,
And how you said someday you'd dive
Right from the highest rock.

We think we are much wiser now
And do what we must do;
But I think we were wiser then,
When I was young with you.

Sylvia Brice

Berlin 1945

Bare-footed children in skimpy clothes,
Clambering over ruined remnants of dwellings,
Searching for things, you know, some of those,
That they can pick up and clean off for selling:
Unbroken tiles, lead pipes, copper wire -
They all are hungry - their situation is dire.

Walking the streets, well-fed and singing,
Occupying forces, in their strange uniforms.
Saying, it is peace, they are bringing.
We are used to bombs, we have seen firestorms.
We are children of war, we know no peace,
Our fathers still prisoners, when will come their release?

War to end all wars - so we were told.
Never again will we be killing our brother.
Such is the wisdom, centuries old.
Man does not learn - we're still killing each other.
For a moment, we amend our ways,
Forget the pain - look back - and call it 'the good old days'.

Helga I Dharmpaul

POTATO PICKING

Potatoes, earthy, rounded, oval,
Smooth or rough,
Unmistakably scented;
Satisfyingly rich and clean.
Fingers stained with brown-ness,
Kneeling, bending, picking, picking
Beneath the rows of wilting haulms,
Serried ranks across the hillside.
Noisy, sweating schoolgirl pickers
Filling hempen sacks beside them.
Out of school for half-day sessions
Released from bells and cramping desks
Into the sunshine of September.

Gymslips briefer far
Than regulation dictate,
Coupon rationing not allowing
For replacement!
Navy knickers peeping 'neath them,
Socks all wrinkled,
Shoes mud-caked.

A reason perhaps for always loving
Taties, praties, spuds, potatoes:
Earth's autumnal offering.

Helen Perry

THE DARK AND THE COLD

Oh well here I go, get it over with,
Get the bath from the outside wall,
I know it's where the spiders live,
Just hope on me they don't fall.

I hope the fire's nice and big,
And that the water isn't too hot,
Or I'll be doing a little jig,
As I carefully lower my bot.

Dad stoked the boiler up I know,
Before he left for work at the pit,
More cold water please Mam,
Before I finally have to sit.

I'm sorry Mam, but I have to go,
I really can't hold it any longer,
It's the sight of all the water you know,
Wish my bladder was stronger.

Off out into the dark and cold again,
Towel wrapped tightly round me,
It really is a heck of a strain,
It's so dark I cannot see.

I've now got whitewash down my arm,
Trying to get the paper off the door,
The flippin' string has broken,
Bits of newspaper are all over the floor.

Well it's off to bed I go now,
Poe in one hand, candle in the other,
Dodging the creaky steps as I go,
Can't wait to snuggle under the cover.

Glennis Horne

DEMISE OF THE BIRDS

In a cottage just a mile away
When I was very small
I found a thrush's nest
Built underneath the wall

Hidden by fragrant honeysuckle
'Neath the dining sill
Five tiny beaks were opened up
Waiting for their fill

A robin made its home
Inside the garden shed
Where a Pyrex dish upon the shelf
Was feathered for a bed

Bluetits flew to and fro
To a hole in the bird table
I watched them coax their little ones
To fly when they were able

I've retired to a bungalow now
High above the vale
A solitary blackbird
Gives voice upon the pale

Rooks come and gather up my bread
The odd sparrow, he may call
But of thrush, robin, bluetit
I see them not at all.

Sheila Scott

THOSE WERE THE DAYS

Where have those good old days now gone?
When open house for everyone
Doors unlocked, folk trusted you see,
Much countryside to roam so free.
Walking and cycle rides the way
Fewer vehicles than today.
Maybe pony or tram to take
Those longer journeys for to make.
Own entertainment, see a show
Lots of laughter, on picnics go.
Outside toilets no mod cons then
Women at home whilst work for men.
Solid fuel stoves and candlelight
Imperial measures that's right.
Ration books and counting the cost
Blackout curtains sirens not lost.
A friendly word as passing by
A cup of tea and apple pie.
Recalling all those bygone years
Joys and sorrows, laughter and tears.

Margaret Jackson

WHEN AND THEN

Before the days of dismal, lonely high rise flats,
Where elderly people can't even keep their old pet cats,
Before the days of snobby semis and aloof modern detached,
Were rows of old terraced houses - all very well matched.
Jostling cheek by jowl, sometimes even backed to backed.
In those days 'next door' always helped out - unasked -
Whenever the need arose.
For each little house door was never locked or closed.
No need to be lonely, for longed for privacy was something
                                    they often lacked.
Then each back yard wall peeped onto its neighbour
And all and sundry could watch each other's hard labour.
Monday's toil of washing blew on every small line,
Wonderfully white, but soon covered in grime -
Nearby factory chimneys belched out smoke all night and all day.
No wonder everything was soon dismal and grey.
But the housewives, undaunted, strove to be clean,
With only set pot, board, tub and dolly. Alas! No washing machine.
Arms and backs ached through turning the heavy wooden mangle,
But then too waists were very much trimmer!
And always on Mondays we were lucky to have even a cold dinner.
For all were poor and work, when found, was hard.
Some were lucky if they ate just only bread and lard.
And when all the coal was used and the range was empty and cold.
We still kept warm, because we wore our coats even though
                                    they were tatty and old.

Margaret Poole

OH, I'D STILL LIKE TO BE BESIDE THE SEASIDE

Do you remember how it was to be beside the sea,
With Punch and Judy on the sand, and tray with pots of tea?
And cornets, tubs and wafers, or Mivvis on a stick,
And seaside rock, the dentist's friend, that made you feel quite sick?

Of changing in the midst of crowds with towel around the waist,
With awkward drawers, and 'I saw yours!' and clothes pulled on
                                                in haste?
Of shivering blue with shoulders wet, on a windy, cloudy day,
Lying on soggy blankets under a sky turned grey?

Of inching slowly down the beach on pebbles sharp as tin,
With slimy clinging seaweed that the playful surf brought in?
Of cuts needing Elastoplast, too damp to ever stick,
And tar from passing tankers, and wind chapped thighs
                                        and sunburned neck?

Of squash that tasted salty, and flies on picnic jam,
And oil that stained washbasins brown, Waspeeze and Anthisan?
Of deckchairs set to pinch your thumbs, wool bathing suits that itched,
And buckets when their handles broke, no chance of being fixed?

And paper flags on wooden sticks, that parted in your hand
Of scummy moats with plastic boats, for castles made of sand?
Until the first high racing wave of each incoming tide
Levelled hard-built fortresses, and badly bruised your pride?

Of rubbing sandals, filled with grit, and rushing back in time
For guest house gong that pealed at seven, summoning all to dine?
It reminds me still of happier days, a child without a care.
The memory plays tricks, I know, for that was forty years ago,
                                        but I still wish I was there.

David Farebrother

CHRISTMAS EVE MEETING

1990

We always meet on Christmas Eve,
Pretend we are very near,
Have a laugh, hold back the tears,
Must send love,
Wishes for a happy day,
Then put down the phone,
So sad I could not stay.

1998

Now so many have gone,
We met for so many years
Over thousands of miles,
Harder still to hold back the tears,
I must phone the children,
Try to make them smile,
Hope we too shall always meet
On Christmas Eve.

Florence Andrews

THE GIFT OF A REAL CHILDHOOD

I loved you Nan and Grandad all the afternoons
       I played in your backyard
Learning to skip, top and whip, digging the muck
out of the cracks in the wall, with a sharpened lolly ice stick
All the Sundays at New Brighton, gripping slimy rocks
         with my red plastic sandals
Ice-cream upside down on the sand, bucket with
     Rupert Bear, sandcastles, a ride on the fair
Days in the park, stale bread carefully clutched
        throwing it to the swans
All down the endless summer holidays, cap gun and hoops
Lending your bike out for sweets, Sunday school treats
Lucky Bags and Arrow bars
Burning holes in leaves, and charring grass with a
       sixpenny magnifying glass
Picnics in someone's backyard, paper bags full
of broken biscuits, lemonade powder in bottles of water
It was worth being five, six, and seven and eight, nine, and ten
Thanks for my hockey stick, bought with your Green Shield Stamps
and my telescope that made the moon
look like the lampshade in the living room
For all these things, and more,
For the gift of a real childhood. Thank you.

Lily Doyle

THE WAY WE WERE

Way back in the good old days
Before PCs and microwaves,
People had to skimp, and save
To buy the things they needed.
Before TVs and videos,
Gramophones were all the go
To wind it up we would all take a turn,
and the words of the song we'd try to learn.

Leapfrog, and marbles were games we'd play,
on a day off or in our school holiday.
Lucky dips, and sherbet dabs,
were some of the treats that we had.

We would light a fire to boil our pots and pans,
being very careful not to burn our hands.
Toilets were in outside huts,
but there were no fear of power cuts.
With candles, and lamps we got along,
and when we felt happy we'd sing a song.

All our washing had to be done by hand,
but if everything went to plan
The weather would keep fine,
so it would get dry in time.
To be ironed when the iron got hot,
it would take a time if we had a lot.

We would put our rubbish in a bin and not a bag,
and cars were something not many people had.
Sometime we would take a trolley bus ride,
for a special day out at the seaside.
Yes memories of long ago,
bring back a certain glow.

Eileen Kyte

CHANGES

Hospitality's sadly a fading grace,
'Share my bread and my meat,
In my house find an honoured place
In which to rest your weary feet.'
Contrast this with the well chained door -
No visitors here after dark . . .
I'd love to get out more,
It's dangerous to walk in the park.
At what point did the open life
Feel a need to look over its shoulder?
Friendship find itself in strife
As feelings seem to grow much colder?
How can we repair this gap,
So that some can break their shell,
Escaping from the encircling trap
To find life now need not be hell?
Perhaps the breakthrough is a smile,
A gesture made without forethought,
Time to stand and chat awhile
Pleasures that cannot be bought.
'Remember' is the favourite phrase,
But memories can be selective,
We tend to forget some bad Old Days
And gadgets that were not effective.
To help the old ones to survive,
They should join up with their peers,
Yet greet the new things that arrive -
Share the wisdom gained from years.

Di Bagshawe

THE NATURE OF THINGS

Things have a habit of lasting unlike
People who grow and change then vanish.
Places, pictures, books, all remain and strike
Chords of memory, for someone somewhere.

In my case it is an old box of paints,
Bought in the years after the Great War
By my grandfather who designed posters
For the Great Western Railway long before -

The days of computer graphics and the like,
But still those paints have remained. I use them
Now when painting birthday cards and such
And watch the same bright colours blend as when -

My grandfather used them in times long gone
In a world far different from my own.

Margaret Hibbert

THE WAY WE WERE

Once there was manners and civility
Now all we get is rudeness and hostility
To open a door for a lady was a grace
Today alas they are closed in your face
In yesteryear, a gentleman would doff his cap
Now won't do it, not to be called a sap
Arm in arm with friends we would walk
Showing friendliness today only gives rise to talk
Neighbours would pass the time of day
Alas the community spirit has gone by the way
Dare you venture into the corners of a park
Where once upon a time people would skylark
I remember pubs full of good cheer
Everyone's eating, who cares about beer
Gone are the days of dustmen with their clatter and din
Now we have tall effigies, namely, the wheelie bin
The chains and padlocks clutter my door
As the crime rate begins to soar
Catching the last bus home is out of bounds
As thieves and muggers are out on their rounds
Remember going to the flicks getting lost in a dream
Only to be woken by the call of ice-cream
Standing to attention for the anthem to the Queen
Reminding us of the once great country we've been.

Valerie Heeley

LIFE IN OUR TOWNS DURING THE 1939-1945 WAR

I was nine when it all began, with my Dad hanging up
black blinds against our windows, and loud-mouthed
'Put that light out!' wardens knocking up the guilty
who were showing chinks of light at night.
Noisy air-raid sirens, Anderson shelters, search lights,
barrage balloons, ack-ack guns firing, and German gifts:
- Aerial doodlebugs and V2s.

We queued for hours outside shops for our food.
Carried gas masks. Admired men in khaki, navy and blue.
Land girls in long socks. Street training exercises by
Fire Servicemen, and Home Guard volunteers.
Read the war losses in newspapers, and Hitler cartoons;
heard lies from Lord Haw Haw on the radio to dispirit us.
Listened to Churchill's speeches, Tommy Handley's comedies,
and 'Workers Playtime', to lighten our lives.

Trainloads of evacuees were sent from the coasts without
their mums. While new ones cried, and cared for them.
Ration books for food, clothes, furniture, and petrol.
Free tins of dried milk, and egg powder for children.
Identity cards. Call up papers and medicals.
Conscientious objectors, and their persecutors.
News of family members and friends killed in action.

Billposters warning: 'Careless talk costs lives'.
Vehicles requisitioned, iron railings removed.
Pregnant women abandoned by American soldiers.
Women working like men in ammunition factories.
Cinemas and pubs regularly full with overworked,
war-sickened people. Then, a single American bomber
dropped the atom bomb, and brought it all to an end.
Hearts rejoiced in all of Britain's war-torn homes.

Ron Thomas

NORTHERN STREETS

Grey streets lined with unsmiling houses
Their curtains tightly closed
Against prying eyes,
And the shoe factory dust
That scratched its way
Through the hair-fine cracks
Of firmly shut windows and doors.

Streets with razor-sharp corners
Where the north wind
Collected torn scraps of old news,
And filled fist crumpled
Brown paper bags
With its cold wheezing breath.
Streets to hurry along clattering noisily

In metal klegged boots
That were always too big,
Or too small until you left school.
Draughty streets that you were glad to leave
For the dirt-trodden alley
Between high brick walls
That led to your own backyard,

With its welcoming flags
Of damp woollen vests
And striped flannel shirts,
Where the cast iron mangle stood
Like a monster on guard,
And an old zinc bath
Hung like a battered shield
Beside the shabby brown paint of the kitchen door.

Mary Ellis

MEMORIES OF MIDDLE CLASS CHILDHOOD

One of four girls, we were great mates,
Wonderful holidays and family dates
We went on a month's summer holiday to the seashore;
What fun and games, and crabs to explore.
I loved bathing and splashing in the sea,
Loud cries of joy would come from me!
Donkey rides, and castles tall,
Who could build the highest of all?
Money didn't worry me 'til my mother died,
Then my eyes they opened wide!
But when only small, cards at 1^d and 2$^{d.}$
I would send to whole form, and they'd send back to me.
If they were away and at Christmas times too,
I loved receiving mail; in fact I still do!
Chocolate machines, only small pence to put in,
And when bar came out, I'd have a big grin!

When war started, a young 14 was I!
Everyone was rationed, 'Oh, me! Oh my!'
A horse's appetite I possessed:
This situation was no jest!
Of course it wasn't; but it wasn't war on my mind
But of the good food on which I once dined.
Though no money worries, I had seen how cash changed,
In values and styles a completely different range.
Tiny silver threepenny bits, farthings, florins too;
Why was this so? My curiosity grew.

But I remained naive, an impractical soul,
'Til my early 30's, then I changed this role;
When my mother died, I was the only one still on shelf,
I'd to buy the food for my dad and myself.

Film prices soared, and went higher in price;
Our family went en masse; an outing nice!
We all went through the panto stage too,
But the magic remained with me, for I still do!

Before TV, a radiogram, before that a gramophone,
Of course, many dance bands on radio;
We were a happy home!

Marjorie Cowan

THE OLD DAYS

Long gone are the days of old
when children were safer on the streets,
barefoot on the cobblestones playing games,
smiling happy, and not showing they had needs.

Old men with clay pipes in their mouths,
and a flat cap on their heads.
Enjoying their smoke as they went to work
their long shift down the mine was a dread.

Hardened like the coalface, imprinted on their brow,
times were really hard for them,
But long gone are those days now.

The children's mothers would gossip
while doing their daily chores.
Putting a meal on the table
was sometimes as hard as the floor.

Food was sometimes rationed,
a meal a day is all they would get,
but those days were more appreciated,
not like today, they are taken for granted.

Niall McManus

THE GOOD OLD DAYS

Up the yard in the dead of night,
or the white pot under the bed.
Those were nights when the owl would hoot
and shadows move on the shed.
Torch and wellies, overcoat,
trust the night's still snowing.
Through the gate and up the yard,
everybody knowing.
Bursts of moonlight, gusts of wind,
newsprint strung behind the door.
Walls with holes where spiders live,
something move on the floor.
Silent whispers, wind in trees,
the dog in next door's pen.
Could be almost anything when one is only ten.
Demons watch and wait outside,
aliens land with a gun.
Come gather your thoughts and concentrate,
just do the deed and run.
But now it's age that's landed,
so, *good old days* or not,
If things were still as things were then,
I'd have to use that pot.

P Jennison

Sunday School

Remembering days of long ago
When I was but a child,
With Mother's help I'd say my prayers
To Jesus meek and mild.

Then later in Sunday School
With other girls and boys,
Hymn singing, bright and beautiful
And many other joys.

Listening to stories
Of Jesus our Lord,
Wonderful parables
And the miracles He performed.

Depicted in attendance stamps
We were given one each week
To stick in little picture books
Our very own to keep.

I have one still, and to this day
Never fails to reassure,
The Lord is my Shepherd
And will be evermore.

Amelia Canning

THE GOOD OLD DAYS

As children we jogged to school
The winters then were very cold,
With ice and deep snow,
But chimney pots stood out in rows,
Where curls of smoke to let us know
That life was all around
And inside coal fires bright, and warm.

Friday night was Amami night
We took the tin bath from the yard
And bathed before the fire, oh! so nice
No central heating then, hot water bottles
We took to bed
Lights went out, too cold to read or hang about.

Home from school, jumping over the blue-stoned step,
    that mothers on their knees had scrubbed
The kitchen smelt of home-baked bread
And brass gleamed around the black-leaded grate
Tea was toast and a fresh egg
Tablecloths, like sheets on our bed
Were crisp and white from starch and 'blue'.

On the open street we played
Not so much traffic then, skipping in the orange ropes,
And chasing the whipping top, with coloured rings
Sometimes a game of hopscotch too,
Just before it got dark,
We looked out for the lamplighter
As on his bike he rode, like a knight
With his lance, his long hooked rod
    the gas he ignited, as happy faces cheered.

Gwen Haines

LONG AGO
(Dedicated to Mum and Dad)

How times have changed, my head's in a whirl.
I remember years ago, when I was a girl.
Sunday lunch as a family,
then watch the afternoon matinee.
George Formby or Old Mother Riley,
Aunts and uncles would come round for tea.

I remember sixpence pocket money,
when Dad came home from work on Friday night.
We'd rush round to the sweet shop,
whilst it was still light.
I remember the front door key, hung on a string,
If Mum popped out, we could still get in.

Then there were holidays, how Mum and Dad tried.
Withernsea, five in a caravan.
Didn't know, it could rain so hard.
Every year, it would rain every day.
All they could afford,
at least we did get away.

Ah, Christmases, I'll never forget.
The sacrifices they made, to give us the lot.
A pillowcase full with toys, apple, orange and nuts.
A table set with crackers and hats.
A tree in the corner adorned with fairy lights
and every year a few would go out.

I remember one year,
when Dad bought a new bauble for the tree.
As we all sat around,
bubbling with excitement was he,
to show us the bauble of gold,
a parcel he did unfold.
I felt so sad for him as he said,
'It's a golden one - oh it's broke.'

We laugh about it now,
but at the time it wasn't a joke.
Yes, I remember times gone by,
Happily, the way we were.
Sadly, the way we are.

Susan J MacDonald

CHANGES

When chips were chips and accompanied cod -
Roast dinner was served as well as God,
When money was kept in a jar in the hall
Available now from a hole in the wall.
When goods were purchased and sent to our door,
Idly we sit by phone order more,
When doors that were open welcoming neighbours for tea
Knew nothing of current animosity.
When reading books was perused with ease,
Big Ears and Noddy - our conscience to please.
When our pen described an event as 'gay' -
It only meant - 'What a joyous day'.
When aids were a visual perception to life,
Now an embodiment of pain and strife.
When outings were fun for the whole family -
Replaced by the lone child watching TV.
When *it* was a game for you and me,
Accessible today! Information Technology.
When roads crossed safely brought us home,
Dare we scarcely traverse the journey alone!
We reminisce and wonder how -
    these changes did occur.
Impending life, tomorrow's fears -
Did we abide the way we were?

Janet Collinson

EDEN DENIED

Were they really so good, those *Good Old Days*?
I remember long summers, heat - hazy with little rain;
and being able to wander the woods with my beloved dog
without fear, way back when. It was good then.
There was less crime - or so it seemed - a time of innocence,
prolonged childhood, gentle dreams. No fridge, no telly, no car.
We watched the Coronation in '53, awe-inspired by the magical screen
that another family owned. We got a fridge the day I passed the 11 Plus,
and a car came later, opening up a whole new world for us.
On the whole, kids were satisfied with their lot.
Our leisure time knew little else but freedom, sensibly combined
with adults' rules and discipline. If you mucked about in school,
you were chastised, sometimes physically.
Parents and children accepted such things.
No one derided or questioned teachers, as they do now -
A child's right to self-expression had not become a sacred cow . . .
Each class in society still 'knew its place'.
Mankind was still dreaming of conquering space.
New-born and dying came and went in God's good time,
instead of the deception of 'in vitro' conception,
or the soul's torment of being kept imprisoned in the body
by artificial means. Playing God has become the name of the game
nowadays. It was all so much clearer, way back when, in black
and white. Colour now highlights our shame,
our loss of common-sense,
the death of pride in excellence,
and endless shades of grey -
that is sometimes labelled 'progress', but which I see
as further loss of mankind's innocence along his way.
Our Eden now denied.

J M Service

NOW AND THEN

In the nineteen sixties my fashion labels were worn on the inside;
Today they are on display - a practice common far and wide -
When I shopped then I used coins and paper money
Today I exchange plastic cards for products - I find this unfunny.

It was nice for coin collectors to display coins from many a land
Soon we will have one Euro-coin - something I can't quite understand -
The Brownies now wish to join the Scouts - to be one of the boys,
We used to love building cardboard castles and dress our girlie toys.

The height of fashion then was to look clean and smart -
Today torn jeans secured with pins are chic - it's sheer modern art!
On television they reveal everything brazenly about themselves
In my day we hid the bad things - afraid to make fools of ourselves.

Even the driving lessons have undergone changes,
    requiring talents so grand,
Before sitting the test you have to produce passports to enable
    you to travel over our green and pleasant land.
'Get a life, you've lost the plot and I know where you're coming from'
    which they now use -
Have replaced the *sixties* 'Come on man, you've misread me
    and I'm in your shoes.

There are so many television channels from which programmes
    you may choose
The BBC and ITV, in my day, were the only ones we could use,
The GCSE has been devised to stretch to the limit the brainiest
    in the nation,
In my day it was rigid and we did manage somehow as we knew
    that it would be our salvation.

The times have changed as they must - we don't expect to stand still,
We have so many gaps in our knowledge which we rightly should fill -
The human mind is complex so what do you expect?
We welcome new technology, and ideas, some good, some suspect.

Margaret Andrews

BYGONE SUNDAYS

I recall those bygone Sundays,
When early off to Church we went,
Had to wear our best hat on our head,
And without breakfast we were sent.

As Vicar's voice droned on and on,
On Mother's arm my head I leant,
My empty tummy rumbled softly,
And I was really sure I'd faint.

At last the final prayer was said,
And with relief we hurried home,
Into the oven went the joint
And soon its sweet aroma filled the room.

Helping Mother peel the apples,
They were a must for Sunday pie,
While Father beats the batter well,
For Yorkshire puds must rise up high.

It was the best meal of the week,
And afterwards a little rest,
Then to the park to hear the band,
All dressed up in our Sunday best.

Thin bread and butter with strawberry jam,
And peaches and cream for our tea,
Home-made sponge and little cakes
With butterfly wings made by me.

Then as evening time draws in
The radio's on for Hymns of Praise,
Mother's joining in the singing,
Father to her hand is clinging,
Oh, the sweet memory of bygone Sundays!

J Scarisbrick

THOSE WERE THE DAYS

Memories still linger of days that used to be,
Far off times remembered with ageing eyes we see,
The pictures painted in the mind of times now gone before,
When as children how we played outside the cottage door.

The little things that pleased us and brought us endless joys,
No electronic gadgets but only simple toys,
And how we ran occasionally for very special treats,
Coupons clutched in grubby hands to get our precious sweets.

Times were good in many ways, but far off now does seem,
Cars were such a novelty and trains all ran on steam,
Growing food to feed us all, working on the soil,
Filling lamps to light the house with paraffin and oil.

Mothers wearing aprons doing laundry in a tub,
Scrubbing-boards and hard green soap giving clothes a rub,
Days were spent in endless toil, never in a rush,
Pails of water carried in, no toilets then to flush.

No television Soaps to watch or videos to play,
Batteries for the wireless were bought from far away,
The gramophone we played at night, records worn and scratched,
Gave us pleasure and much joy that could not then be matched.

Alister H Thomson

EHEU FUGACES LABURTUR ANNI

Alas! The fleeting years slip away (Horace)

High above my infant head
Red hot pokers - Oh! how red!
      Brighter than the sunset rays,
      Brighter than the bonfire's blaze!
But now they only grow waist high
And barely catch a passing eye -
      I'll plant some out in twos and threes
      And then admire them - on my knees!

John Urwin

BEFORE

In times gone by we lounged and lazed
On days when summer's sunshine blazed
    Caring not for life was fun
As through the winding streets we'd run
Laughing shouting chasing fears
    Happy in our childhood years
Batting balls with youthful might
In cricket clothes of gleaming white
While Grandma's bony fingers knitted
To keep us warmly winter kitted.
Mouth-watering smells of baking bread
Mother's floury pinny and turbaned head
Under skies of blue comradeship strong
Oblivious as the years rolled on.
One day adorned in work's attire,
Extinguished was the carefree fire.
Foundations of our lives were laid,
When we were young and laughed and played.

June Harman

GRAND FINALE

I remember when
I walked down Baden Road
To the Regent Cinema
To watch George Formby films
And Gracie Fields
And how we roared with laughter
Even long after
Remembering their antics
And the News Reels from Pathé News
Designed to inform, not confuse
Telling us about The Battle of the Bulge
And the Big Push
And later, D-Day
And its aftermath
After VE Day when the allies
Had conquered the Hun
And victory in Europe was won
Seeing the skeletal Jews
Those still barely alive
Or able to walk or talk
At Belsen and Dachau
And other concentration camps
And Hitler's bunker in Berlin
But the Japs still refused to give in
Finally seeing an atom bomb
Dropped on Hiroshima
And the huge mushroom-like ball
Overall
And then the Japs
Gave in at last.

W B McDade

WARTIME DREAMING

In our street,
beyond a row of tiny 1930's semi's,
lay a piece of wasteland
where we war-torn children played.

By day,
turning our backs
on pig bins, shelters,
and the static water tank,
we played at hospital
and mums and dads.

At night,
as the sirens wailed,
we stumbled, sleep-filled,
into damp and musty Andersons,
and remembering long-dead days,
dreamt our father's
home again,
our lullaby the slow *pop pop*
of the Bofor's gun
in a nearby park.

All was not so clear to us then.

Doreen Dean

THE WAY WE WERE

Black woollen stockings
And laced-up leather boots.
Elastic under chin to hold
A hat no face would ever suit.

A pencil case, a skipping rope,
Then off to school we'd run,
Along the lanes with every hope
That school had not begun.

Sums and tables every day,
Recited them each morning.
The cane was there if you did play
On teacher's desk, a warning.

No good running home to Mother
To tell her of our misdeed
For she would then give you another
Telling that was what you need.

Home again for dinner
Mother always waiting there,
Treacle pud and rabbit pie
Made with such loving care.

Games we played, whip and top
Shuttlecock and battle dore,
Snobs, statues, skip and hop
Didn't ask for anything more.

Happy was our childhood,
We could play anywhere.
The way we were was good to us,
You see Mum and Dad were always there.

Dorothy Wilbraham

SELF-ASSESSMENT

Self-assessment - what does it mean?
Headaches, heartaches and expenses.
These new tax laws are inflexible.
Made to inflate the government's purse,
while *our* finances go from bad to worse.

Ministers say the system is fairer
and it *may* be for all of them,
but for us lesser mortals it's a nightmare.
Worried frowns crease our brows.
We'd like the past back instead of now.

Wake up all you tunnel-minded MPs,
wake up from your sad old sleep.
Think of the hardships the poor endure.
Change your man-made laws to suit us.
Don't let man sink on that runaway bus!

Daf Richards

UNTITLED

The good old days,
they where the good old days.
How often have you heard that said?
Only from those who had 'lived' them
from times gone by.
To this generation you have to explain
what were the so-called good days.
It was a life without violence or crime,
for life was based on honesty and trust.
What a pity that all that has changed.
Now you walk in fear when walking the street,
watching all the time for a would-be thief.
Gone are the days when people to each other were polite.
Who can blame them, they are just afraid.
The old days were full of sharing and caring,
hard work and clean living that was the way.
Even if you did not have much,
you did not complain.
Without the shame of stealing you got by.
Yes, indeed they were the good old days.

H Birch

CHILDHOOD MEMORIES

Memories of my childhood, how different things were then,
With no electric cooker to do the baking in.
An old black range to heat and cook,
The chimney often filled with soot.
Bread, scones and apple pies the aroma filled the air,
With Grandma sitting knitting, in her rocking chair.
No automatic washing machine to help our mother out,
our clothes she washed by hand and rinse, then wring the water out.
We kids would fold the wet clothes, then put them through the mangle,
one of us would pull them through, while one would turn the handle.
No carpets lay from wall to wall like we have today,
just floorboards stained and polished, each and every day.
Rugs made out of old rags lay upon the floor
Curtains made from blankets hanging on the door.
A tin bath in the parlour were once a week we'd bathe,
From water boiled in pots and pans on the kitchen range.
We children slept in one big bed to keep each other warm
And to hold each other, when there was a storm.
One day a new invention came into our lives
A box called television that we all watched with pride.
We no longer played at Ludo, Monopoly or Snap,
Because this new invention put paid to all of that.
I remember all the children came from down our street,
To sit upon the floor to watch this great new treat.
Now we sit and watch TV, it's no longer such a novelty,
A part of everyday life with all these modern things,
But I still remember when there were none of these.
There tucked away inside my head that's full of memories,
Memories of those long past days and not these days of ease.

Patricia Ratcliffe

NINETEEN TWENTIES TO NINETEEN NINETIES

The good old days, it was like living in heaven, everywhere,
You could not answer your parents back, not aloud to swear.
You could leave both doors open and go out the back,
Anyone came they would walk threw the house, and come
and have a chat.
Toilet was outside from the house, fifty yards away,
When sitting in there snow would blow in there, on a winter's day.
We had yo-yos, they were made of wood,
String tied in the middle, it would go down, unwind,
and then come back up again, it was good.
We would run to school, alongside a hoop of iron,
Hitting it with a stick to make it go along.
Another day would spin a wooden top along the road,
Hitting it with short stick and string to make it keep spinning
and jump like a toad.
When we went to school, if we saw two cars on that day
We were lucky as there were all ponies and traps those days.
In spring a small lorry with two men putting sand aside of the road,
Heaps five yards apart both sides of the road.
Then came one horse pulling a tar pot on wheels,
A man would, with a pipe, spray tar all over the road.
Then a gang of men with shovels would take the sand off the heaps,
And spread the sand all over the road.
Then a steam roller came along once,
The front roller did the middle and side wheels did the side.
The roads were just as wide as a cart in those days.
When my mother went to school, there was grass in the middle,
And gravel where the wheels go.
I know of a road today that has tarmac where wheels go,
and grass in the middle.
It's in the village of Burgh St Peter, in Norfolk.
Our school had three classrooms; infant, junior and senior.
Three playgrounds; girls, infants and boys.
We started school at four and left at fourteen.
Playgrounds, were gravel in those days.

Our playing field used twice-a-week sports centre for fifteen
to twenty-five year olds, free, Tuesdays and Thursdays from 7pm to
10pm

There was football, netball, tennis, baseball, deck-tennis, cricket
and volleyball, all played on playing field.
We only went to one school in village of Saint Lawrance.

E M Thompson

A WORLD AT WAR

The Germans bombed our ports so bad,
They 'hit' our 'chip shops', that was sad.
The Allies clambered underground,
As air raid sirens 'wailed' around.
Blackout all your windows, the 'blitz' has come to town.
Dive into your shelters,
As bombs come 'tumbling' down.

As war got worse black market thrived,
Then ration books were thus subscribed.
Make do and mend, dried milk, and egg
Corned beef and spam would do instead.
Re-pulp your waste, your paper,
To make the cannon shells.
The 'privy' down the garden,
Has news sheet, (hard as nails).

Our women worked in the factories,
On buses and trains, in the Land Army.
Some watched the fires, some nursed the sick
With their gas masks ready, should they need them quick.
Lord Haw Haw told 'Big Stories', propaganda was the word.
We watched our fronts, we watched our backs,
Not believing all we'd heard.

Our Home Guard they were standing by,
Their weapons polished, and spirits high.
We'll meet again sang Vera Lynn,
Victory was sweet and we would win.
'They don't like it up 'um, so end this awful strife.
God save our King and Country,
And give us back a 'life'.

Heather Overfield

CHILDHOOD

Playing 'Knock Down Ginger' was a game that brought us fun,
Once we knocked we all tore off, at our fastest run!
We didn't have a park you see, but this we used to find,
The games we played made us use our wits as well as mind.

Castles, forts, maybe a shop, whatever you did think
Perhaps a submarine, from which the enemy you'd sink.
The battlefield was debris, where once a house had been,
But bombs that had been dropped on it, completely changed the scene.

We didn't have a TV set, we didn't have a car,
And if you had a holiday - you didn't go too far.
One thing that everyone possessed, where'er you went it seems
In common you would always find - each one had their dreams.

But now with our technology, computers and the like,
Children don't play 'Five Stones' or go out on a bike.
They don't need to invent games - as we used to do.
But I'm glad I had my childhood years - just after World War Two.

Letitia Snow

CHILD OF THE FIFTIES

Winter frost has laced the glass inside my windowpane,
Hurry into knitted vest, long woollen socks and tie.
Liberty bodice, vyella blouse and tunic of blue serge,
Creamy porridge fills the bowls, all night it's simmered low.

At school the chanted tables drone, the milk is served from cans,
The squeaking horse on rusting springs stands by the folding screen.
Dividing infants from their kin, the juniors' upper class,
Warm chalky air and coke-filled fumes enhance the learned scene.

Savings stamps of Charles and Anne, bean bags and cod liver oil,
Raffia mats and card milk tops, woolly balls made by the ton.
Line up for dinner with bakelite plates, some bring Oxo
                                    lunch tins from home,
Intoning grace with bended heads, while a pea flies through the air.

Hurrying home past hedgerows deep, parting prayers ringing round
                                    in our heads,
The table laid with bread and marge, blackberry jam and real
                                    rind cheese.
Potatoes baked in the ash of the grate, and tea from the brown china pot,
All lovely and warm neath the dolly head crown and her billowing
                                    knitted skirt.

The oil stove casting shadows of glimmering rosy red,
Dancing in a pattern of flowers above my bed.
Hot water bottles with flannel coats are tucked beneath the sheets,
To warm my chilly winter feet, as into bed I leap.

Helene G Ford

MY GRANDMA

I can never remember my grandma just sitting,
She was always sewing or doing her knitting
From early morn 'til after dark
She would always be busy with her work.
The washing to do in a great big tub
With bars of green soap and a brush to scrub,
Her hands were always rough and raw,
The soap and cold water would make them sore.
The bubbling boiler belching steam,
What would she think of my washing machine?
No TV set ever ruled her home,
No fridge or freezer or even a phone.
She bakes her bread and pastries and cake
A big stew for dinner she'd often make.
Eleven children born in her big old home,
But she loved them all with never a moan.
When people talk of the good old days,
If she could live now, what would she say?

Sheila Wells

OUR HOUSE LAUNDRY BLUES

Nowadays, there is no hustle, bustle or quandary,
When time arrives to do the laundry.
It is so simple to regard, I may say
As any other day not now to view with hostility.
With each modern facility, it is a day much like any other,
But how very different it is now child's play,
Unlike washing day in the time of your grandmother.

Firstly she sorted out the coloured from the white,
Then left them to soak, in soap suds all night.
In the morning separated the dirty from those only soiled,
Then commenced them to boil, the dirty were then scrubbed.
Before being deposited into the dolly tub, for this was her washer,
Then agitated manually with a hand-held posher.
Then as she aughta, she exchanged the hot water,
Next thing she thanked the Lord, for her ribbed scrubbing-board.
Then each item received a rub and a scrub,
As with energy she did push her special scrubbing brush.
Next job was about, wringing by hand out as much water as one can,
Then each item to untangle before passing it through the mangle.
Then was the time to peg out on the line to hope and pray,
The weather would remain dry today, for no one had any desire
To bring them back indoors to dry by the fire.
Grandma found it all so trying, next to warm with the heat of the fire,
Her flat iron certainly it was so trying.
For the rest of her evening she would be ironing,
Then of course, onto the clothes horse
Located where the laundry could air, there to stay.
Anyway, until she will put them away.

B Howell

PEOPLE SAY

The good old days people say
But were they just well no way
Walking behind a horse all day
With an outside loo down the garden far away
Before tacking up the horse before I could start work.

The good old days people say
With ration books and five hungry kids
How could you dig for victory in a town
With a lot of houses and no spare ground.

The good old days people say
With just a radio no TV
A man in black what did he say
Just a lot of work and sweat.

Keith L Powell

DAYS OF YORE

The Good Old Days were trod
Full of emotional gifts
Of love for your neighbour
Not a case of sadistic drifts.

One had to work hard
But laughter always prevailed
The days of 'When will we eat',
Marred life but, thoughts of soon, triumphed!

Chickens were given a year's grace
Not killed when young to satisfy our race
Lambs were happily playing together
Then lived in style until lamb chops were light as a feather.

Mutton was a Sunday dinner special
The old ones were killed to meet our trivial
Wants but, animals were loved
By their owners and daily fondled.

A day at the seaside
Was a wonderful treat
Looked forward to for weeks
On end, the tide of happiness was great.

Life was lived more leisurely
No rushing around almost out of one's mind
But time to see God's gifts pleasantly
Arrayed, in spite of the dark mills, factories and mines,
                                    things like that kind.

Oh! for the open fields
Instead of brick and concrete monstrosities of today
When one could see the stars in trillion at night
And watching the moon in its splendour in flight.

We had time to love and adore
Worked hard, yes, but we were never a proverbial bore!

Alma Montgomery Frank

THE WAY WE WERE

At seventeen I met a friend
At work in Lincoln's Inn
The war carried on - and so did we -
Never giving in

We typed all day
From nine till five,
And gave thanks that we were still alive

Life was busy working queuing, air raids causing many sensations
The landmines, one at the back of our house in Medburn Street
Running down the road in bare feet

In winter we went to work in the dark
And came home in the dark

Good evening you would say
To a little torch coming your way
That is all we had to see with
'Til the light of day

Just imagine, we dreaded the beautiful moon
Like a great big torch in the sky

We came home to wonderful meals regularly
Sarah Georgina (Mum) was so organised
She would never say if she was tired
She managed the rationing so well

Peaceful were the days - except for Hitler
I still remember the beautiful summer weather

Our friends made a pact - it we were to survive -
To meet in peacetime, somewhere bright and alive
But life goes on, and we lost contact -
I wish so much that I could bring them all back

Phyllis O'Connell (Hampson)

YESTERYEAR

When I was young
I had to watch my tongue,
do what I was told
or else they would scold.
It was left up to you
what you wanted to do.
If you played with the budgie
or used the outside 'cludgie'.
To buy sweets you got a penny,
this of course would buy you many.
You daren't be bad
or he was waiting, your dad.
On Sundays we watched television at Gran's
of Perry Como we were great fans.
Just a little boy not very tall
oh how I laughed at Max Wall.
I ran from school as fast as my body
so I would be in time to watch Noddy.
Great to watch The Wooden Tops
or laugh at the Keystone Cops.
Then on Monday morning time for school,
in those days you daren't act the fool.
You could not be late even if the rain did pelt
because the teacher had a great big belt.
Then at the end of the day
you were glad to get away.
So home to Mother
she made the tea for me and my brother.
Then by Dad, a story was read,
before you knew it, it was time for bed.

Frank Tonner

ECHOES FROM THE PAST

He sat forward in his wooden chair,
One leg in the hearth, one on rumpled matting,
The fire lit up his old grey eyes,
Dancing, like his legs in former days.

He stared down at his hands,
Hands that dug trenches, mended roads,
Survived two wasteful wars,
Reared a large family.

Those same hands, though frail today,
Wielded in their prime, picks and shovels,
Lifted heavy stones, shifted coal,
Inflicted penal rule.

He reflected, as he watched the flames,
How life had changed since early days,
When horses graced the roads,
And only birds flew in the sky.

Running hoops along the street,
Hopscotch on the path,
Skipping ropes and humming tops,
Glass marbles, smooth as silk.

Yule logs on the open fire,
Hot buttered toast for tea,
Reading books by candle glow,
Warm feathered eiderdowns.

As he filled and lit his briar pipe,
The old man closed his eyes
And to himself he reminisced
How times were better then.

Keith Withey

MIDLAND OUTING

Go down by Victoria Street where ancient station stands
Your ticket bought in ticket booth, newspapers from The Strand
Dinner in the diner, coffee from a pot
Breakfast from the tea bar, where you 'ad it bought

You might 'have had Salvation Hall, if only you 'ad thought
Cups are given out in there, without it being bought
Gone to see the palace, that's the place to live
If you're there on Maundy Morn, money you they give

Keep your 'ands in pockets, everywhere you go
That will show the spivs, Midland people know
Hear police band in the park, it plays there every day
Criminals love to hear it, while they get away

Watch the guard on horses, round at their parade
After they have gone, see the cannon aid
Go round Seaman's Mission, watch the tide come in
Smelling like the brewery, they 'have all been in

Look in at the cathedral, very nice within
It's even nicer outside, they say it's free from sin
Go up postman's tower, don't eat when you are there
It will cost you lots of money, and it don't fall out of air

Now all that's free in London, is in Trafalgar Square
But only when the pigeons have taken to the air

W Robertson

WHERE?

Where is the coal to light the fire?
The only fire in the house.
The scuttle is empty, the bunker is bare,
We're as poor as the proverbial mouse!

The coal is still in the station yard
Little more than a mile away,
But who will offer to fetch a sack
On a cold and icy day?

There is no car to carry the load,
Nor a cart, or pony and trap,
Just a rusty pram with crooked wheels
That's been thrown on the heap for scrap.

Where is the carpet to cover the floor,
And the duvet to cover the bed?
There is no carpet to keep our feet warm,
Just a threadbare mat instead.

'Where is the meat for the Sunday roast?'
You can hear the children cry,
- There are only vegetables, freshly dug,
For another carrot pie!

Oh for some chocolate creamy and rich,
Or a biscuit with sugar on top,
But the coupons are spent and the rations have gone,
And there's nothing left in the shop.

But where are the woods and the cooling streams,
Where we used to play in the sun?
Gone are the woods and pretty wild flowers,
Along with the laughter and fun!

Janet Jones

THE WAY WE WERE

I remember playing out in the street
When a pennyworth of fades was a special treat
And the lamppost was used to play games of cricket
It was sturdy and strong and made a great wicket.
We made our own games up and all joined in
Diablo, Statues, even kicking a tin
We read our comics over and over
'The Wizard', 'Lark', 'Hotspur' and 'Rover'.
We had no telly or video game
And discipline in the classroom was done by cane
We always felt rich with just a few bob
Everyone shared, there was no need to rob.
Our doors were left open for neighbours to pop in
Nobody worried if they were fat or thin
We didn't have hamburgers, we had stew instead
While our kitchens smelt of home-made bread.
A holiday for us was a trip on the trains
We didn't have computers, we used our brains.
And the reason our memories are recalled with pleasure
Is because the love in our homes was held like treasure.

J Gilchrist

THE BAD OLD DAYS

Compared with everything today,
Way back when I was small,
Come birthdays and come Christmas time
Our gifts were nothing at all.

We might get snakes and ladders
That we'd play with mum and dad
And sometimes a wind up clockwork car
And some sweet mice they weren't bad.

'Cause we never had a telly at home and nobody round owned a car,
But we'd all sit and listen to Children's Hour, or go for a walk,
Sometimes far.

We only had the countryside, not a great big fenced in park,
Yet of course we could always play hide and seek,
For hours when the village was dark.

I'd never heard of a skating rink
There were some in the cities, I s'pose
We all had to slide on the local big pond
Every winter whenever it froze.

We never had dinners at our school
We had to walk home to our mum;
Course she had to be there, all day all the time
To see to our needs when they come.

But now with the cars and tele
And the house built behind a brick wall
I reckon that I had much more then
When I had nothing at all.

Gerald Burr

My World

In my world
There's only love to see
In my world
Life's like eternity
In my world
There's no trouble or strife
Not in my world.

In my world
There's a welcome everywhere
In my world
Love is always in the air
In my world
There's no hatred or spite
Not in my world.

In my world
There's no lock and key
In my world
Everyone comes to tea
In my world
You won't hear a lonely cry
Not in my world.

In my world
Call in, I'm here for you
In my world
There's many things to do
In my world
You will always find me there
Yes, it's my world
Just say a simple prayer.

Roland Powell

A SIGN OF THE TIMES

Gliding upwards on the escalator
in the department store,
I find myself on the second floor,
stepping off into a field of silk, taken unawares,
lace panties, satin shifts and
brassieres.

Reluctant to linger long among lingerie,
I move on upwards where
the men's attire might be;
and realise that word
is now quite rare -
for the female garment called
the brassiere.

If used today it might
be taken for a restaurant.
Or one of those strange metal things
which watchmen filled with coals
to warm their bones,
before the invention of fluorescent cones.

Like so much else these days
the word's been dropped;
a trend unfortunate that
can't be stopped.
Just one short ugly sound -
the beauty of the thing remains
but not the word, whose ring
with mystic beauty shone;
abbreviated - sacrificed
upon the altar of convenience -
all the mystery gone.

John Mercer

THE WAY WE WERE

I remember, when I was small,
Grandma had brown lino on the floor.
My icy bedroom did not invite my presence.
Our 'blackout' curtains a dread to me,
As I couldn't fathom why?
Specially, when I heard the sirens,
And saw the arc light in the sky.
The cinema queue stretched forever,
As grandad's hand I held.
After the two films and news in black and white,
Every person stood and sung,
The National Anthem to our King.
It was an automatic thing to do.
Then, out into the thickest of fog,
Not a hand could be seen in front of our face,
It was a very scary place.

Mary Wain

THE WAY WE WERE

On a hill in Ulster long, long ago,
cottages were built for ex-servicemen so.
Vimy Ridge they were called and we loved them so.
To be children, of those gallant men, who fought long ago.
To school, we walked every day and we were happy
in our own sweet way.
The Second War came and it was great,
the Belfast children came and we stayed up late.
No locks on the doors and dry toilets too,
ration books did us for groceries few.
My dad dug the garden and kept us well fed,
and mum she baked us good soda bread.
My dad kept the windows well covered at night,
so they didn't let out any light.
And Jerry planes crossed over too,
and we said our prayers and hoped they passed on through.
Now the days of yesteryear were great,
God meant me to be there,
it was my fate.

Marian Kerr

BRIXTON, THOSE HAPPY DAYS

I was the boy, who worked in Bill's café,
With Charlie, and Johnny, always good for a laugh.
This was Brixton you see, in the year '36,
When kids used to play, 'Knock 'Em Down, You Win Six'.

Those happy days, when we walked to the shops,
At Christmas, the lights, lovely snow, such a lot.
Great Expectations, like a new pair of boots,
But as dad always called them, 'the old daisy roots'.

Hackford Road School, the masters, and boys,
On return after Christmas, would discuss all the toys.
No jealousness then, even though some had none,
The Salvation Army, made sure you had fun.

Soon would be New Year, what would it bring?
All things bright and beautiful, the hymn we would sing.
So very few cars, on the roads, in those days,
Children could walk, without fear, anyway.

Adults were trusted, if you lost your way,
Delivering newspapers, brought you some pay,
There was sixpence for mother, and sixpence for you,
This helped all the family, to buy food, or some shoes.

Yes, life was so happy, although it was tough,
It you told children today, they would answer,
            'Too rough.'

A Powell

The Way We Were

In the olden days when we were young,
In some ways, materially, times were harder.
Food was rationed, with very little in the larder.
Grandpa walked to work at dawn.
Ever regardless, sometimes of feeling fresh and bright.
Each morn, when time was tight,
He was up with early daylight,
So home where everyone loved best,
Had time to be used to eat and rest.
For crime people had no wish or energy or time,
They only counted sheep, ready to prepare for
An excellent night's sleep.
With loos outdoors, going for a 'wee' was deadly
Uncomfy, on pavements and hard, cold floors.
Everyone helped others in severe need, or there was
Time to chat to neighbours about families and news,
To sit and listen and to respect others' views.
Even when you sometimes disagreed, the subject of
A chat often turned one's mind to its 'learning seed'.
Communal spirit, help between neighbours,
Made for 'welcomes', when doors were opened in a
Friendly manner and the neighbour had,
Plenty of tea or coffee in t' pot (as they say in Yorkshire).
Now in 1998 time is so rushed, and everyone
Is pushed to achieve deadlines for their tasks.
For more time for the pressing jobs, we need to ask,
Time now is far less leisured, and in some ways
Not treasured, so modern progress makes us
Sometimes laze, and think back,
'Oh for those, in some ways, wonderful days.'

Jean Davy

WHEN WE WERE YOUNG

Oh how I remember, when we were young,
the things we used to do, to make our
own fun, we would get an old bicycle
without any tyres, and ride it around,
and have fun, for hours and hours.

And after school, at the end of the day,
we would all go down to the farmer's yard,
and slide down his hay. O' yes I remember,
when we had a lamp on a stand,
no water taps, but an old pump in the
back yard, you had to pump by hand.

But now those days have gone,
as with each passing day,
as we are left with only memories,
of how things used to be,
when we were young.
My friends and me.

Raymond Wakefield

PRIVYTISATION

This tale concerns that little house
That's been called so many things.
One often shared it with a mouse,
    With commoners and kings.

Do you recall those halcyon days?
    That box upon the floor,
The only light, some spare sun's rays,
    Through the crack above the door.

Think about that white scrubbed seat,
    How water raised the grain,
    Be very careful how you sit,
    Those splinters give such pain.

Remember that string you had to hold,
    To keep that damned door closed.
How miserable when weather cold,
    And the chilly east wind blows.

Those torn up squares of Daily Mail
    For your convenience there.
Hanging from a three inch nail,
    What pains we had to bear.

Thumbing through those paper squares
    You pull two from the nail,
    One to use, one to peruse
    Then drop them in the pail.

We mustn't forget the accompanying sounds,
The tinkling of the pee,
The mighty rushing of that wind
As finally it breaks free.

Be grateful for these present days
With bidet, shower, so neat,
Oh! how we like these modern ways,
With bathrooms now en-suite.

Fred Foster

THE WAY WE WERE

I was born in '38
Surprised to find I still feel great
Post war days I do deduce
Had ration books out in full use
Sweets were limited, as well I know
And to the neighbours' house I would frequently go
To ask if they required their ration
And if not, then 'Please could I have them?'
Bananas also spring to mind
To see them at all was hard to find
When nana wanted just a few more
Our greengrocer would 'find' some at the back of his store
Quickly into nana's bag so they would not be seen
And her treat to us would be bananas and 'milk' cream
Money for the 'flix' was also rare
And I have to confess (my mother would have despaired)
Round the back of the Odeon our young gang would go
With coat hanger in hand to the exit door we would flow
Our leader would fiddle and fuss with the door
And then it would open and in we would pour
Up in the balcony we would secretly sit
If the management knew, they would surely have had a fit
Times must have been hard, but my siblings and me
Had such happy times and ignorant were we
Of what our kinsfolk had been through as difficulties grew
Our parents' love and caring for us was all that we knew
Oh happy days of yesteryear
It flies by so fast, what's that, oh dear, it's a tear.

Brenda Wickstead

THE WAY WE WERE

No water laid on - we had to fetch it from a running spring
¼ of a mile down the road.
No electricity - but oil lamps.
No gas.
No indoor toilet - a man came round once a week with a
horse and cart at midnight to empty it.
No rubber hot water bottles to keep you warm at night,
but a hot brick wrapped in newspaper, sometimes it used to scorch.
We used iron saucepans heavy like a ton of bricks.
A giant mangle with huge rollers.
Flat irons with a protective tin cover over it.
We used to heat the iron first on a stove then put the cover on
and start ironing the clothes. Some people didn't use a cover,
the iron itself was a bit rough sometimes.
We had a galvanised iron bath, water had to be fetched and heated up,
then we took it in turns who had their bath first, the rest of us followed,
'What a horrible thought.'
Tramps used to knock on our door, asking to fill an old tin can with
tea or water, and had we got an old piece of dry bread to give them.
We used to give them something, they were grateful.
Sometimes one tramp used to sell bootlaces.
Gypsies often came knocking on the door selling old fashioned pegs
that they had made.
The rag and bone man used to bellow out 'Rags, has anyone got any
rags or bones or any rabbit or mole skins for sale?'
Our baker used to come round with a horse and cart.
On Good Friday he used to come round as early as 6 o'clock am to
deliver real 'hot' hot cross buns, they were gorgeous.

Amy Barrett

ROMANTIC SEDUCTION

A table for two, candles aglow,
a tablecloth white as snow.

Wine sweet to lips so divine, do meet mine,
legs touching beneath the table,
hands clutching tight, all night.

Speaking softly words of love,
eyes laughing bright,
darling hold me tight.

Bodies trembling with delight,
feeling you will be once more mine tonight,
as you are every night.

Children of love fast asleep
finding words we seldom speak.

Remember how it used to be
when we first met, beside that old oak tree.

A romantic seduction, was it then, you said,
you would be mine, till the end of time.

Paul Volante

THE GOOD OLD DAYS

I would give up many things of the modern, everyday life
Once again in the way we were!
When I was a young boy I used to go out every night
And the front door of my house was always open.
No one would rob you of anything
In those old days there wasn't theft anyway
And the people were so friendly in every street
Everybody used to have a long chat with their neighbour
And all the doors were open
Because the people used to talk to each other all the time.
Today nobody chats anymore, they lock themselves in
Because they feel strangers to each other and they're all scared
And it is why the doors are all locked with specially reinforced locks.
This is the worst when you can't trust your neighbour.
If God asked me to go back in the old good ways
But I had to give up all the modern things, I would say yes
To return and live friendly lives.
We all lost the communication with our neighbours.
My neighbour says only 'good morning' and 'good evening'
And that is it and the good old days are lost forever.

Antonio Martorelli